Sweet Dreams Ohio

Adriane Doherty • Anastasiia Kuusk

Rubber Ducky Press
Indianapolis, IN

The sun rises as eager eyes open up to a new morning. We are going to explore Ohio searching for adventure!

The flags fly high at the Ohio Statehouse in Columbus. The building is made of limestone, and inside we can learn about the art and history of Ohio.

The Columbus Park of Roses is in full bloom.

It is a beautiful day to take a stroll down the streets of German Village. First, we'll stop to eat, then we can visit the local gift shops and bookstores.

The Red Stable

The National Museum of the U.S. Air Force is the oldest and largest military aviation museum. It is full of all kinds of amazing planes, spaceships, and uniforms from different time periods.

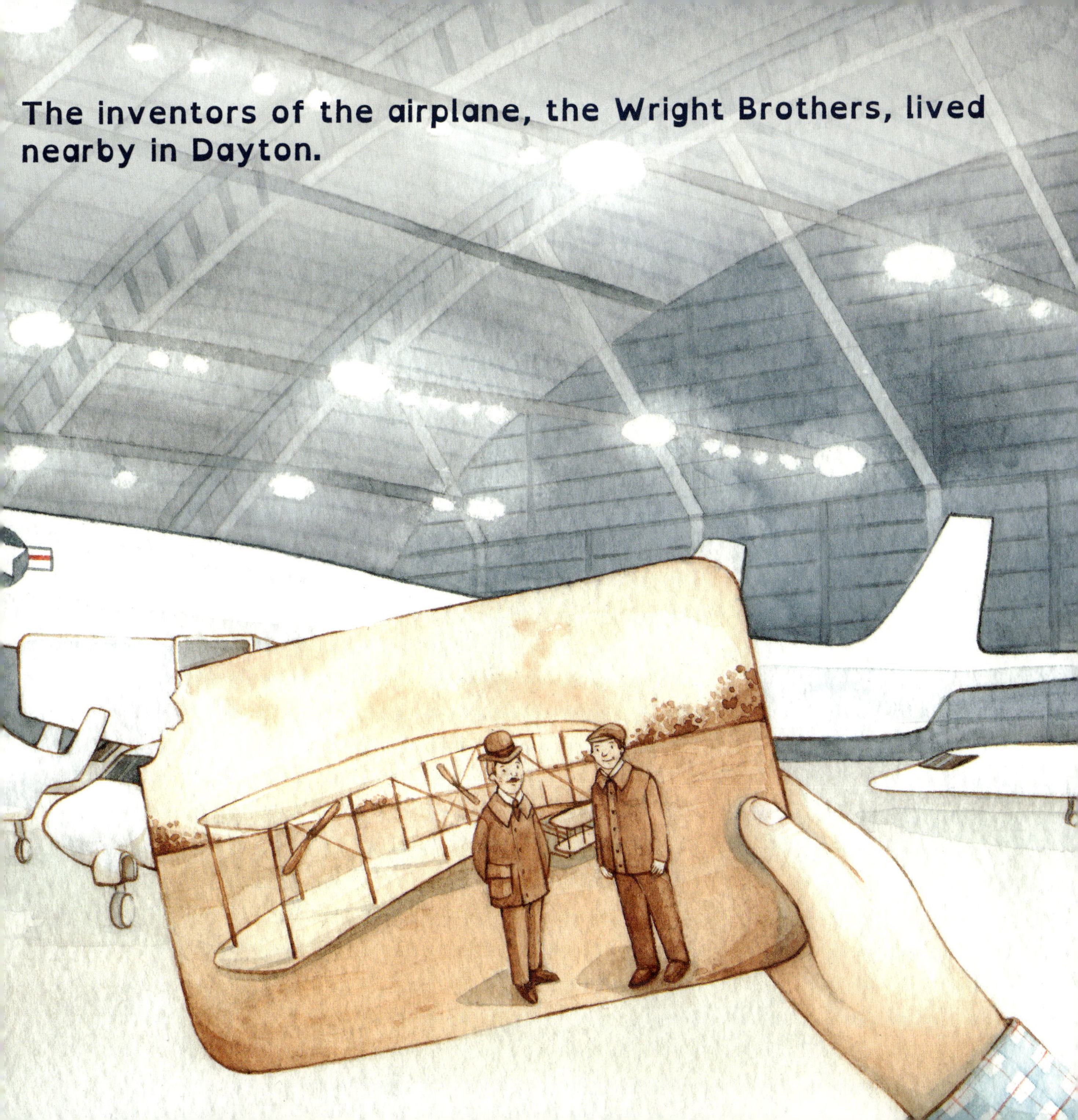

The inventors of the airplane, the Wright Brothers, lived nearby in Dayton.

At the Toledo Zoo and Aquarium, the snow leopards sun themselves as visitors pass by. Across the way, the flamingos enjoy the cool water on their long legs.

At Nickel Plate Beach, along the shore of Lake Erie, we can play in the sand and build sand castles. Maybe later we can walk to the lighthouse or go fishing off the pier.

The sun shines bright as the ferry boat pulls up to Put-In-Bay. Off in the distance, we can see Perry's Victory and International Peace Memorial standing tall.

While at Put-In-Bay, we decide to spend the day at Perry's Cave for an underground adventure.

The Cleveland Museum of Natural History is a popular place for field trips.

Students can see giant dinosaur bones, learn what a fossil is and how they formed, and talk about how nature has played a role in shaping the state of Ohio.

CLEVELAND METROPARK
CUYAHOGA VALLEY
GREAT PARKS of HAMILTON COUNTY

Ohio has many great parks. At Hocking Hills State Park, everything is so green. A momma duck and her baby ducklings gracefully swim by. A picnic near the waterfalls is always nice.

A fun way to see the countryside is to drive through the rolling hills of Ohio Amish Country. We decide to visit a working farm. Every year we look forward to taking a wagon ride, going to the petting zoo, and shopping for fresh-baked pastries.

Along the Ohio River Scenic Byway, we find a place to run and play with our friends. Good thing Mom doesn't mind if we get a little wet in the fountain!

CINCINNATI
NATURE
CENTER

At Cincinnati Nature Center, some white-tailed deer stop for a drink of water. "Hello, deer family," a young Ohio Buckeye says gently, trying not to scare the deer away.

Back in Columbus, the children start to grow sleepy as the family heads home from a day's adventure at Franklin Park Conservatory.

Sweet dreams, family.

Sweet dreams, Franklin Park Conservatory.

Sweet Dreams

After a day of exploring, we are all cozy and looking forward to a bedtime story. Thanks, Dad, for reading us our favorite book.

Sweet dreams, explorers.

Wow, what a busy day!
I wonder what we'll do tomorrow.

Sweet dreams, Ohio.
Sweet dreams, everyone!

Where in Ohio did we go today?

Download a free parents' guide at rubberduckypress.com

e amount of Farmland utilized each year
ies, but typically Ohio has about 14
lion acres of farmland available to farm
Ohio's more than 75,000 farms.

e Ohio Statehouse Rotunda (Columbus)
a remarkable sight, stretching 120 feet
m floor to skylight. The Statehouse also
asts a museum and many works of art.

lumbus Park of Roses features a large
riety of plants, including a species of rose
at dates back to the Roman Empire.

rman Village (Columbus), originally
tled by mid-1800s German immigrants,
today a popular destination for shopping,
ing, and strolling.

tional Museum of the U.S. Airforce
esents military aviation history with more
an 360 aerospace vehicles and missiles,
d thousands of historic items.

ledo Zoo is home to more than 10,000
mals of 720 different species. According
the Library of Congress, it is sometimes
led "America's Most Complete Zoo."

e current Huron Lighthouse near Nickel
ate Beach was constructed in 1939. Its
at can be seen for twelve miles.

ring the winter, the population of Put-
Bay drops to only 480 people. While the
urists are there, it can average as many
50,000 people.

Cleveland Museum of Natural History is near the Cleveland Museum of Art, Botanical Gardens, History Center, and Children's Museum.

Some of the first Ohio public parks in the late 1800s featured reservoirs for Ohio's canal system. These lakes became the first of Ohio's State Parks in 1949.

Ohio Amish Country, an area northeast of Columbus, south of Cleveland, and east to the Pennsylvania border, has something for everyone with shops, farms, and museums.

The Ohio Scenic Byway is 452 miles long and spans 14 Ohio counties. Along the way are many attractions like state parks, museums, and President Grant's birthplace.

There are lots of places to learn in Cincinnati like the Cincinnati Nature Center, Cincinnati Zoo & Botanical Gardens, Newport Aquarium, and Krohn Conservatory.

Franklin Park Conservatory (Columbus) contains a community garden that produces over 3,500 pounds of fresh fruits and vegetables each year.

In the bedroom, a hippo toy lays near a dollhouse. Fiona, a very popular young hippo, was born at the Cincinnati Zoo. She even had her own television mini-series.

The world's oldest traffic light is in Ashland, Ohio, and Ohio was actually the first place to use firetrucks, ambulances (both Cincinnati), and police cars (Akron).

Adriane Doherty

Adriane Doherty read to her young children daily, and her love of books and helping young minds grow and understand the places around them inspired her to write the Sweet Dreams series. Adriane has explored Ohio with her family from Lake Erie to Columbus to the Ohio River and many places in between.

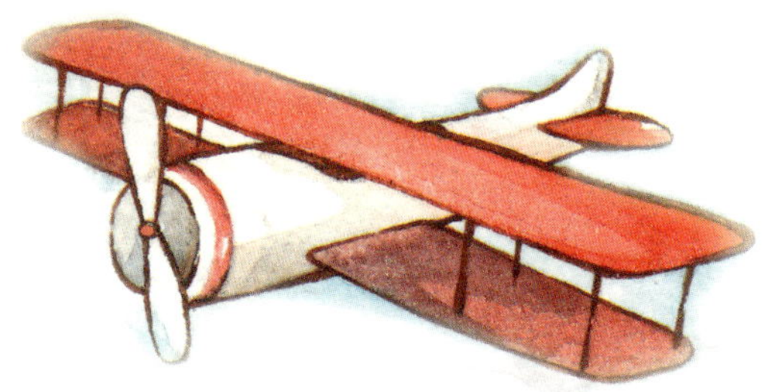

Other Rubber Ducky Press Titles You May Enjoy:

ABC Christmas

ABC Indiana

ABC Michigan

ABC Ohio

ABC Texas

ABC Yellowstone

Sweet Dreams Chesapeake Bay

Sweet Dreams Indiana

Sweet Dreams Chicago

Goodnight Sleeping Bear

Find coloring pages and puzzles at rubberduckypress.com

Distributed by Cardinal Publishers Group, cardinalpub.com. Printed in Hong Kong.